Brother Elephant

Written by Sarah O'Neil

Illustrated by Meredith Thomas

Flying Start
to Literacy®

Contents

Chapter 1:
Disaster in the desert

"It's time to go," said Jamil to his camel. "It is a long way back to our village."

Jamil reached for the last thing he needed to pack – his water bag.

But when he lifted the water bag, he saw a long black snake. Jamil dropped the water bag in fright.

"Go away," he yelled at the snake.

The snake moved quickly towards the camel. But if there was one thing the camel did not like, it was snakes. The camel jumped away from the snake.

"No!" yelled Jamil, but it was too late. The camel landed on the water bag and all the water spilled out.

"Oh no!" said Jamil. "I will not survive for long in this desert without water. What will I do? We must get back to our village as quickly as we can."

Chapter 2:
At the river

Jamil set off with his camel.

Soon he saw some trees. As they got closer, Jamil saw some plants growing along the banks of a river.

"We are saved!" he said.

But when they reached the river, there was no water. The riverbed was dry.

"Plants cannot grow without water," said Jamil. "There must be water under the riverbed. If I dig a hole, I will find some water."

Jamil dug a hole in the sand,
but he didn't find any water.

He dug another hole
and then another hole,
until he could dig no more,
but still there was no water.

He lay on the sand
and closed his eyes.
Soon he fell into a deep sleep.

Chapter 3:
An old desert elephant

While Jamil was asleep, an old desert elephant came down to the river.

The elephant sniffed the sand as he walked along the dry riverbed. Then he began to dig a hole in the sand with his trunk. He could smell water.

Jamil's camel began to push Jamil with his nose.

"Stop it," said Jamil, but the camel did not stop.

Finally, Jamil sat up.

"What is it?" he said.

And then he saw the old desert elephant. He was putting his trunk into the hole in the sand and then into his mouth.

"The elephant has found water," said Jamil. "I am saved."

As soon as the old elephant finished
drinking, Jamil ran over to the
hole and drank and drank.

"That elephant has saved me," he said.

For many days, Jamil and his camel followed the desert elephant as he travelled along the dry riverbed.

When the elephant could smell water under the sand, he would dig a hole with his trunk. Jamil would fill his water bag and drink some water.

"This elephant is looking after me,"
said Jamil. "He is like a brother."

Chapter 4:

Home at last!

At last, Jamil reached his village. The villagers came running out, shouting and waving their arms.

"They have come to welcome us home," said Jamil.

But then he saw that the villagers were carrying spears. And the villagers were pointing their spears at the old desert elephant!

"Stop!" cried Jamil.
"You must not hurt this elephant."

"This elephant has come to steal
our water," the villagers cried.

"There is lots of water in our well,"
said Jamil. "We can give some of our
water to the elephant."

"Why should we?" said the villagers.

"This elephant saved my life," said Jamil. "I was in the desert without water and this elephant found water for me."

Jamil told the tale of how the elephant had saved him, and the villagers were amazed.

From that day, when elephants came
to the village looking for water,
the villagers would say:
"Welcome, brother elephant.
Welcome, sister elephant.
We are glad to see you.
Please drink some water with us."

A note from the author

Desert elephants are such big animals and they need lots of food and water, yet they can survive in the desert. The people who live in the Namib Desert – where the desert elephants are found – have a special relationship with them. They call them brother and sister elephant, and this caught my imagination. How had this come to be?

I began to imagine what might have happened to lead to the first time that a person called an elephant his or her brother, and the story for *Brother Elephant* began to take shape.